ah

RACHEL KELLUM

ah

Poems by
Rachel Kellum

Liquid Light Press
Premium Chapbook First Edition

ISBN-10: 0983606382

ISBN-13: 978-0-9836063-8-3

Liquid Light Press

poetry that speaks to the heart
www.liquidlightpress.com

Cover Art by Rachel Kellum
Cover Design by Tom Maroshegyi
Back Cover Layout by M. D. Friedman (*mdfriedman.com*)
Photo of Poet by Kit Hedman (*kithedman.com*)

Contents

From the Poet 1

Where Words Wait 5

If You Want Silence 6

To Meet Your Mouth's True Mother 7

No Metaphors For 8

Waking into Sleep, Take Your Waking Slow 9

The Machinery of Desire 11

Desire Builds a House 12

Vision of the Great Mantra 13

Eukaryote 14

Clear 15

While It Happens 16

Listen 17

Hopeful Ruin 18

Then Dive 19

Conch 20

Look between Breaths 21

Exodus 22

Detachment 23

To Everyone I Tried to Eat, I'm Sorry 24

Sutra for Poets Who Would Be Buddhas 27

Reading You 31

Tapihritsa/Liberation 32

Dedication Prayer 33

for all sentient beings

From the Poet

These poems were born of a year of daily Dzogchen practice in the Bön Buddhist tradition of Tibet. Prior to this, though I had studied Bön for nearly eight years, my meditation practice had been a bit sporadic or rushed. I suppose I believed, like most Westerners, that there wasn't enough time for such slowing. In the summer of 2011, however, I took a break from teaching and dedicated myself to practicing every morning for an hour in my garden and again in the evening before bed. I was astounded by the changes I felt happening in me, and when the new school year began, I found I had made a habit I could continue through the year.

Most of the poems in this collection were written shortly after my Dzogchen sessions, usually seeded by impressions that arose during practice. It was a challenge to relax into nonconceptual awareness while sitting in my usual word stream, and a relief to realize a great space was opening in me where words could arise and dissolve naturally. Off the cushion—and sometimes on—I might catch or be caught by them and begin a poem.

I didn't originally set out to write a book of poems. I was simply intrigued and inspired by a set of practices my teacher had given me: *The Pith Realizations of the Great Perfection*, a collection of poetic instructions—some might even call them poems—pointing out the experience of natural mind. Kindly, ancient Zhang Zhung Nyen Gyu masters wrote down these once strictly oral transmissions that are now shared more openly by 21st century teachers in an effort to preserve this endangered tradition. I was intrigued by these poems because poetry seems like the perfect

1

vehicle to carry out the paradoxical task of illuminating the nonconceptual through the conceptual and inspired because I wanted to give it a try myself.

Engaging with their words took me places I couldn't resist translating into poetry. I share my own words not as a master, of course, but as a Western student and poet playing with imagery that suggests my experience. My hope is these poems will be of benefit to not only Buddhist practitioners, but also anyone interested in engaging with the rich space of their own awareness. I'm grateful to Markiah Friedman of Liquid Light Press for inviting me to gather these poems for publication, for believing that poetry serving human consciousness with an attention to craft is worth printing.

The sky image on the cover is an oil painting called *Sky Mind* that I painted in the same year these poems were written. The calligraphic symbol is the Tibetan syllable A, pronounced "ah," which represents spaciousness. Enclosed in a circular prism, it is the traditional visual support for an introductory meditation practice called zhiné that helps stabilize the mind in calm abiding. I created this image of A in a calligraphy workshop with Tenzin Wangyal Rinpoche, my root teacher, whose compassionate dedication to making Bön practices accessible to Western students has made my deepest joy and this volume possible.

Where Words Wait

When I am nearly quiet
and perfect words appear,
silence is more perfect.

I tuck the precious phrase
behind my ear like windy hair,
or gum to save for later chewing.

I promise words a quick return.
My most important work requires
such wild undoing: an empty mouth.

If You Want Silence

don't seek a quiet place.
         Let trains   rattle and call
dogs   howl
the freeway hum   the rain
                  fall
         in ticks
     and taps
         the movie mumble
through your
         bedroom floor.
         It is not necessary
     to close
your doors.
         Just listen to the lacy din
     or each sound
in turn
     the way you'd notice
         a cloud   or   bird
drifting,
         then   shift
to the blue   behind.
         Fall in.
Silence lives   in the shape
         around sound.

To Meet Your Mouth's True Mother

all

                   she requires   is a quick

dive

into   background

      a sliding   swim around

mind's   bobbing

                             words.

      Once she receives you

do not wonder how

                you've always missed

her

        ever awaiting

your timeless

     warm   return.

No Metaphors For

Say hello to the great shining
embroidered with your fleshy personality.
(The shining may be a clear hole, but if that scares you
think instead a rimless, bowlless, friendly bowl.)
I pull at our tight threads with poems.

Unraveling, I talk too much.
I'm paid to tell you what I know, but there are holes
in knowing funneling toward the shining hole,
and you fall through. I can't catch you.

You can't catch me.
We think our words are handholds,
or that our hands are words, but they are only bumps
stalling speed so fast it's empty, so vast
even the sky falls through.

Waking into Sleep, Take Your Waking Slow

You wake up a sphere
of clear crystal and the bed
is in you. The blinds shoot

curved through your belly
and light glints where
there are no eyes.

You roll out of bed
and surprising legs lift
you, hands touch

your belly, shoulders
open, tangled hair
catches still

air, and the invisible
eyeball itches,
now two.

You scratch their edges,
rub with clumsy fists. Blink.
Shuffle to the toilet, the mirror.

And the flesh's uncertain
and certain longings begin
knotting the endless net

of thoughts by which you
organize your day into
that which you

want and don't want
to fall through you. This
is the morning's way.

with thanks to Roethke, Emerson and Tenzin Wangyal

The Machinery of Desire

1

Everything is calling, clicking
an intricate clockwork of longing.
Crickets rub their toothy wings,
cars race hungrily along black ribbons,
airy arms tingle for breakfast,
pigeons ever gurgle on the wire,
dogs whine to be let in—pity them,
and me, I chase my stories round
my head looking for the end.

2

My words are never content with silence,
that great engine churning poems.
And why not? Silence has everything to say,
everywhere to go. Words are its wings
rubbing together, singing come here, love me,
leave me alone, no—stay, yes—go, listen, don't
look too hard for me. I'm under the pile
of dirty jeans, I'm tucked in the crotch
of the mulberry tree, I'm up here
in the mouth of the great horned owl, waiting.

Desire Builds a House

of me for you to live in.
Doors are everywhere.

The walls are roaring
flames sucking stale air.

You can't enter.
I burn myself out.

You'd never know
a house was ever there.

Vision of the Great Mantra

The lazy, dozing deities
and dull knived killers
of my body

the whining pin throats
and misled, missled gods
of my body

the leg humping dogs
and hand wringing humans
of my body

wear every single cell—
each a full body halo
gone orb rainbow

in the great eye
of my body.
There is no place within

I can't wake. I walk
through the congregation
of my body

like a forest
where everyone sits
under trees half grinning.

Eukaryote

when there is too much to do
this quiet temple
wrenches in terrible mitosis
quaking to split
into two hearts
four arms
nine eyes
excavating
sky

Clear

this clear column
of sky,
my subtlest spine,
opens
a funnel through
my crown—
the rest of me
dances
around it, holding
hands

While It Happens

Don't think about it while it happens,
that slippery moment
buckthorn dreams your spines and deep berry eyes
while a neighbor dog barks from your chest.

Notice, don't think, the ever twirl.

Thyme breathes your nose,
your eight palms: cupped basil leaves
out reaching each other for sun.
Comfrey knits the bells of your tongue
to sweet kneed bees.

Church bells ring your eager skin a church,
calling all in. Heavy, your peony head arches
to earth, petals wilt on your flagstone feet,
your thin neck clutches a fist of fat leftover seeds.

Don't think metaphor, personification or make believe.

Don't think.
This isn't the work of similes
or even cosmic permeability.
Rest. Stop swinging
the lamps of your body.

Listen

The world requires doing and noise.
And when doing slows,
and sound,
sound moves around inside. We want
to follow
where it goes and get
lost in a decade old desire—
blue eyes
just before the mourning dove
kiss, or
in the mist of the next decade when no
young boys
will thump through
the silence
holding them like a mother who listens
and knows why
there is war in the world.
We cannot
stop it, and neither can she,
these ornaments of silence, ringing.
We can only notice spaces
between, silence
underneath,
hold them,
release.

Hopeful Ruin

Looking for what is holy in my aversion,
I close my eyes to take in the burning
of my inner bureaucracy, plastic hallways

puddling in a maze. I leap through oxygen
of a most stubborn desire—the fuel
of my decade-long moment of hopeful ruin.

Then Dive

clouds crawl in around the head
guts turn three shades darker

swim cavernous looking for light
sparkle beneath the body's water

Conch

Tell what marvels roll on grey tide.
Don't throw the shell back to sea.
Hold it to the ear, bloom wide.
Spiral, spread pulse into the blue.
Wind inward rainbows, pearlized.
Saw off your tip and blow.

Look between Breaths

Tiny seed of stillness on the peak.
Tiny seed of silence in the valley.
We are born enormous space in each,
edgeless gods sucked into a wave.

Exodus

My left eye wanders
from what my right eye dreams.
In the mirror, it is a wave
parting in the middle of my face,

my own red sea. Two peoples,
one fleeing, one in chase, both
ignorant, unseeing, make
a pilgrimage from my head

into the cleft of my cathedral
chest where everyone fingers brown
bodhi seeds. When the waters mend
their seam, no one drowns.

Detachment

You've walked in like a worldless god
and claimed me as your home.
How is it these arms cannot hold?
How is it this hair needs no tangled hands,
these thighs no tremble? Whose breath is this?
Are you a demon or an angel?
You, wordless, whisper, give it all away.
At once I am an onion cliché, peeling back and back
in your hands. And there are no tears
for what falls: couches, hair, clothes,
trinkets, houses, a rainbow of countless gods,
no tears to find that, smaller
and smaller my core is enormous
eventful emptiness that watches
and waits to be passed through.

To Everyone I Tried to Eat, I'm Sorry

I have chased mountains
and quiet men, wolf women
and booky teachers:
Help me!

I've been every mother,
frowned
and stomped for silence
hoping it would
point.

Even so,
my throat's
been
so thin nothing
could pass, my abdomen
immense
globe of hunger stretched
around boundless
ache,

wandering ghost belly.

No woodsy cabin or bear man
fed. No singing or dying
woman,
witch or nun could satisfy
with wands or words
or all the grief
I could eat.
I had it wrong.

Only when in uncalled dream
I found one hovering just above
no within
no as
(me) unadorned,
clear as ringing
goblet

casting
prism mandorlas
did lost paths merge.

My belly turned inside
outward,
swallowed me
along with the spinning
world
and everything
was perfect, of one
taste.

It fades, this flexibility.

Sometimes I walk
around allowing all
passage,
my human throat and belly
a ruse for the fact
that the path to this
much space was
never any
where or who
but here.

Sutra for Poets Who Would Be Buddhas

Stitch shut the million mouths of books.
Find a smiling teacher, still alive.
Become as trusting as a child or bird.
Stop flinching, doctors, masters, sleeping
children, dear hearts, perched on the edge
of your self, dreaming of wingless flight.
We will not be graded on a curve or for creative twist.
There is no need to be the teacher's pet. Stop fawning.
We must do what is taught and only trust at first;
experience has not yet bred our confidence.

Notice your hesitation. Notice you are a mess.
We've read hundreds of books and still are fully dressed.
Listen. Follow, just this once. It can't hurt to try. Proud
EuroAmericanScholarPoetJudeoChristianIndividualistCapitalists,
we've believed the books we bought are enough!
But know this: they have never walked through doors
of scorching anger or burned with blue desire.
Books have no faces, sex, hands, breasts or beating hearts!
Secretly, we believe in bellies more than alphabets.

Here is the hard part, the poet's heresy:
Stop worshipping words,
especially your own, for just a moment,
for many moments. Every morning for life.
(Here they come again! again! atomic cockroach words!
ever waxing gibbous words! whispering, spoiled
school girl words! billions of blinding sunrise words!)

Regardless of what the Good Book says,
the Word is not your flesh. Of course, it is, but isn't.
It is wind. Just like flesh, but trickier. More subtle.
Flesh remembers before words do.
Pain lodges first in flesh.
Start here. Look.

All that pain. Incessantly we've talked
about it thinking it will help. It doesn't.
(So you were dragged to a small cow town,
so you broke your braided vow,
so you traded your child's now now
for a fuller bank account.)

See how the words spin axle deep?
Words can't talk you out of you.
Stop talking to yourself.
Get beneath your marvelous story.
Learn the colors of your own ancient winds.
Watch them swirl and pass.

You will cry in your bed
when the sky finally falls upon you,
into you, through you,
when you realize neither your own shining idea
of enlightenment, nor your best poem,
nor your oldest moldy book was enough
to save you from your handmade map,
your precious night, your one-eyed fear.

We've been so proud. We lost years reading,
lulled into thinking we got Jack's It.

Dry your tears. It isn't in books. It is you. Sit.

Sit on the ground in front of someone—not me,
friend—who can introduce you to your own mind.
Not your smart ego that bosses your dumb one around—
you've already met a million times, Tenzin said—
but the sky-mouthed one beneath,
laughing through your stories' clouds.

One story: I didn't want a teacher.
But now you have one. Surrender.
He knows the sky-mouthed one in you
inside before you do, will teach you:
spine straight, neck long, hands folded
jaw loose, tongue relaxed, eyes closed, heart wide.
He points to your wordless, lineless lines.

You sigh. You see.

Then you become the sky book you read.
The key is familiarity. Sit.
Under stars and buzzing alley wires,
in the dark morning's artificial lights,
in your grim windowless office,
over the sunken sorrowed grave,
next to your sleeping lover, aging dog,
any where, every day. There is time.

The more often you read yourself
the sooner your stories fly off the page.
Words become locust sound and starling waves.
Pain becomes five dancing prism lights,
every one a grinning doorless doorway
into quickstarred space, your heartbeat sky.

Then you realize the fuss you made
about bowing to a teacher was a waste.
When you bow to him, you bow
to your own seamless cosmos nature.
He knew this from the start and
tricked your pride. Humble now, you pray
to your own clear mind. You are the teacher.
You are the book beyond flames.
You can no longer put yourself down.

Reading You

Write all
you sense

upon clear
strips, line

by line.
Lay each

one upon
the next,

hold this
stack up

to sky—
try to

read it.
Give up.

Be read
by sky.

Tapihritsa/Liberation

When the thing you wanted becomes the thing
you don't want, and the thing you didn't want

becomes the thing you want, you begin to see
problems do not live in things, but in wanting

and not wanting. If you could throw away
your jewelry, let down your long hair, burn

your clothes—you've seen blue jeans burn red—
and sit unadorned in your own invisible colors,

all things could dance through you without a snag.
You would almost smile, but not quite, and the mouths

of the earth would pray to you for insight. You
would grant nothing and everything. The two

are the same in the way wanting and not
wanting are the same. It is best to simply offer

your utter nakedness to those who
wear the clothes you left behind.

Dedication Prayer

May any good that walks
through the three
doors of me

walk toward
your three doors.
And yours. And yours.

Once we leap over
stones of who we were,
are, or could be,

burn through clouds
of clench, shove and sleep,
may we quickly wake

the internestled light
of our three prism bodies
where we are less than one,

more than three

About the Poet

Rachel Kellum lives on the eastern plains of Colorado where she teaches writing, humanities and art classes at Morgan Community College and chairs the visual arts program of MCC's Center for Arts and Community Enrichment. Her poetry has been featured in several online publications, including *Barnwood International Poetry Magazine*, *Four Corners Free Press*, *Blood Lotus*, *Slow Trains* and *The Telluride Watch*. In 2008, one of her poems was nominated for a Pushcart Prize. Most recently, Rufous Press featured two of her poems in the international collection, *Lush*. Kellum performs her poetry around Colorado and blogs at *wordweeds.com*, where you can learn more about her background and read her latest work. *Ah* is her first book.

Other Books from Liquid Light Press

Leaning Toward Whole, **Poems by M. D. Friedman**
(Released June, 2011)

This poetry chapbook from the international award winning poet, M. D. Friedman, contains pieces both poignant and personal. *Leaning Toward Whole* speaks to both the universal and the everyday, both the moment and the millennium.

The Miracle Already Happening - Everyday Life with Rumi,
Poems by Rosemerry Wahtola Trommer
(Released December, 2011)

Rosemerry Wahtola Trommer's superb collection of poems, inspired by Rumi, is full of heart, humor, peace and wisdom. This chapbook gracefully flings us from our routine into the joy of life, bristles with surprise and dances with mystic vision.

Spiral, **Poems by Lynda La Rocca**
(Released March, 2012)

Award winning poet, Lynda La Rocca, creates a compelling poetic and melodic discourse from the persistent cravings and fears inside of each of us. This book is both as darkly sweet and satisfying as chocolate and as nourishing and healing as mother's chicken soup.

From the Ashes, **Poems by Wayne A. Gilbert**
(Released June , 2012)

Master jazz Sufi poet, Wayne A. Gilbert, chronicles the loss of his mother with powerful, bittersweet honesty to create this beautiful collection of poems that is universal in its scope, transcendent in the depth of its understanding and exquisitely musical in form.

All Liquid Light Press books are available directly from
www.liquidlightpress.com **both in print and as e-books or from any of the current major global distribution channels including Amazon, Barnes and Noble, the iBookstore and the Ingram Catalog.**

www.ingramcontent.com/pod-product-compliance
Lightning Source LLC
Chambersburg PA
CBHW021916040426
42447CB00007B/880